# The Unpredictability
# of Light

# The Unpredictability of Light

*Poems by Marguerite Guzmán Bouvard*

Word Press

Published by Word Press
P.O. Box 541106
Cincinnati, OH 45254-1106

Typeset in Adobe Caslon by WordTech Communications
LLC, Cincinnati, OH

ISBN: 9781934999400
LCCN: 2008942696

Poetry Editor: Kevin Walzer
Business Editor: Lori Jareo

Visit us on the web at www.word-press.com

## Acknowledgements

With gratitude to the magazines in which these poems first appeared:

"Chloe" in http://www.genesko.com

"My Town, "One Body," Step by Step," "Invading the Mountain in Combloux," and Weaving a Web," in *The Journal of Kentucky Studies*

"The Important Thing" in *Confrontation*

"As Dusk Fell" in *Poet Lore*

"Brazzaville" and "Always" in *Hawai'i Pacific Review*

"Sister Water" in *The National Catholic Reporter*

"Learning to Read" in *The Midwest Quarterly*

"River in Spring" in *The Connecticut Review*

"Mer de Glace" in *Barrow Street*

"In Transit" in *Poetry Bay*

"Names" in *Doe Press*

"The Second Tide" in Anthology, *What The Sea Keeps,* Bayeux Press

"Faith" and "Reprieve" in *Lalitamba*

"The Shape of Light" in www.TheRavingDove.org

"Only on This Earth" in *Passager*

"My Grandmother's Blanket," "Where They Put You," "Maud," "The Years" in www.womensvoicesforchange.org.

"Vera" in *Louisiana Review*

"Praise", "View from the Future", "Under the Rain, "Red Bud", and "St. John in the Desert" appeared as an electronic chapbook in the *Santa Fe Broadside* under the title "The Intimate Lives of Trees."

"The New Barbarians", "What Words Can Do", "In Praise of Flowers", and "My Country" appeared in the *Santa Fe Broadside* under the title, "Shattering the Silence."


Photo by Jacques Bouvard
Cover design by Jacques Bouvard

With special gratitude to the Virginia Center for the Creative Arts where most of these poems were written and for its unfailing support.

# Contents

**View from the Future**

The World that Flames Around Us

# Ana

You gaze at the bush outside the window
of your tiny apartment, telling me
it throbs with birds, that it is winged
and filled with secret doors.
You soar with those birds
as they twitter among the branches.
You fly beyond the time of secret gatherings
under Batista when your life hung
in the balance and when you fled
the country you loved for the second time.
You fly above the long year
of your brother's dying, above your grown children's
sudden storms. You are sloughing off the skin
of discord and of the insignificant.
You are pared down now
to the blue waters of Varadero, the papayas
glistening in your father's garden,
the poems by Ruben Dario where nothing
can be destroyed. Weightless,

you are what you were meant to be,

wrapped in wonder, your eyes

brimming with the unseen.

# Blessings

*for Valeria Guzmán*

Because she bought me books
when we had no money:
fairy tales from around the world,
astronomy books I took to her office
on Saturdays when I was only eight years old
and pretended I understood.
Because she took me to museums
when we had no money
and when we had a little more
she bought me a kiln
never minding when I scarred the rug.
Because she bought me books,
for Christmas, letting me choose
so I could learn my own lessons.
Because she let me be,
let me spend hours gazing
at the trees stitching earth and sky,
the mysteries unfolding from galaxies

of buds while she came home

from long days at work only to begin

again. Because she always kept the windows

open and never shut doors,

or tried to make me stay,

my mother is still there: her gentle voice,

her strong hands still guiding us all,

and also the trees, the maples'

jeweled arms in fall,

the elms inscribing their blue

calligraphy over snow,

the wonders spilling out

as she bent over her drawings

and her old singer sewing machine.

# Balance

The slow, woozy drone of giant bumble bees
criss-crosses my open door.
They are ferrying nectar.
They are building nests and mating.
It is spring; rustle of wings,
ricochet of bird-calls,
they do not know the text
*conquer and subdue*,
only the web and litany
of the Creation; stamen, pistil,
hive, haven, putting by
for lean times. They whir intently
on their miniature engines,
circling above me. They mean
no harm. They do not poison the air.

# Dominion

The truck geared up and hauled off her calf
as if we had dominion.
Who is to say that only humans
can love? All night I heard the cow
bawling for her calf. All night
the cows huddled together, knowing
theirs would be next. Who was it that wrote,
*the Great Chain of Being*, a pyramid topped
by humans? Have you ever seen cows
burning and pillaging? They are devout: they read
the book of earth daily, tamping down ridges
in the highest mountains to make a path,
gathering beneath a lone tree
under high noon as they shudder off flies,
bearing the brunt of endurance under heavy rains.
They do not have to learn patience.
They are not lesser in God's eyes.

# My Grandmother's Blanket

Rather than her diamond ring, her silver
filigree bracelet set with corals,
I cherish the blanket my grandmother
brought with her from Trieste.
When I make the bed, I love turning up the corner
of that soft camelhair where her initials
are sewn in, A.D for Anna Dejak, or *Anno Domino*,
my mother would quip. I still sleep
between her embroidered linen sheets,
part of that same trousseau.

Her maids stirred them clean with paddles
in tubs of boiling water
while Nana visited with her friend Maria
remembering their schooldays
at Sion in that sitting room
with parquet floors.

The blanket's satin bindings
are long gone, the edges frayed.
I could sew on new ones, make it more
presentable, but it reminds me of how we live
and survive, ricocheting between chaos
and order, tears and ecstasy.

Nana not even thirty, a war widow
with a young child, moving into her father's
house on Via Palladio, wearing black
for a year. Dark-eyed, with a manner
that could charm or cut
she turned her back to suitors,
loved only once.

Nana, alone in her apartment barely
two decades later, the German soldier
banging at her door and she
all height and dignity,
 replying in flawless German,
 "You have the wrong address."

I keep her camelhair blanket
on my bed, to give me her warmth
and courage as I swing between
the order and the daily wars
of my life. Always I see my grandmother
traveling across the ocean and arriving
in our household as if she had just crossed
the street. I see how quickly she learned
a new language, our strange ways,
walking through our town
her head held high
as if she had lived here all her life.

## Mer de Glace

We stood at the glacier's edge:
not a sea of ice,

but a stunned river
its gravelly roof studded with boulders.

Space caught us
in its wings, and the glacier's blue-green

chasms painted by algae.
Then we all crowded into the train

for the valley: Germans and Swedes, French
and Japanese. The pines blurring,

the clacking wheels lulled us
until an elderly man boasting

about his feats during the War,
addressed my husband

in German. "I am French,
I lived through the Occupation,"

my husband flared. "I lived through
another kind of occupation,"

the man spat out as we plunged back
into our own histories.

# The Shape of Light

*for Uwe Jonas*

Today in the Church of the Ascension in Germany
over 60 years after the *Final Solution*

when all but a few pastors bowed
before the Third Reich

a young artist has plunged his hands
into the muck of history.

In the broad aisle between the rows of pews,
he has arranged mosaic chips

to form a Jewish star with one of its points
severed, the scattered pieces off

to one side, a wound we may choose
to honor now when we bow

before our God. The faithful walk carefully
around it as they come and go

before the altar. In that soaring space
with yawning windows

they must look down not up. In a world
that still keeps trying to tear us asunder

may we become mindful of our steps.
May we make our present time more bearable.

## Vera

      In my dream were rows of people
in black shrouds. There must have been hundreds.
There was a deep silence at the service
because you had dismissed God
when you were only 15 and Prague was flooded
with Nazi soldiers. That's when you began to pass leaflets
out at school, when you began teaching languages
to the German Colonel's daughter to gather information,
and carrying two passports in your pocket
as you guided Jewish families over snowy paths
through a countryside where you knew which door
to knock at and how. That's when you climbed out
the bathroom window to escape the soldiers
guarding the door and when you were finally caught
and brought to Auschwitz.

      Your teeth were knocked out
as soon as you passed through the gates.
A friend recognized you and ordered you to scrub

the shed. *Keep scrubbing* she yelled.
When you were done the others had become
wreaths of smoke.

When you were 19, with the Allies
closing in, you were sent on a death march.
You escaped and hid in a haystack. The farmer
demanded his price. With a group of former prisoners
you commandeered a car, painting it with a red cross
and roaring into the camp to gather documents
before they were destroyed.

I will always see you standing
in the classroom in that blue polyester pantsuit,
holding a thermos of coffee as you lectured,
always hear you telling me you never worried
about things like lost keys now. And I still hear your wry
humor when someone asked *What's the biggest problem
in America today?* And you replied,
*stupidity.*

Those last years when you were

on oxygen you funded new scholarships, mentored students

from your wheelchair, sent books to a library in Shanghai.

There was singing at your funeral. You had taught

a young friend the Czech national anthem.

You who had lost so much — your only son

killed in an accident, your husband of 50 years

now dead — kept guiding people through the woods.

Your god was your quick mind, your overflowing heart.

# The New Barbarians

Envoys didn't crowd the horizon with their ships
or trample the plains on horse back.
There was no jingling of spurs,
no wind gusting against our doors.
When they arrived, mothers
were driving their children to school
and the man across the street
was loading his golf clubs
into his car, the grocer was stocking
his shelves with cereal boxes
and the dress shop manager
was changing the display in her window.
When they arrived our ears were tuned
to our own footsteps, our thoughts
bounded by our ordinary days. Men
in well-pressed suits and carrying briefcases
slipped from their high-rise offices
and entered the wide open gates
of our city. This was no Troy

no Jericho. They spoke to us

about new dangers. They told us all

would be well now and we believed them.

They spoke a language

we thought we understood, assuring us

we would be safe now

from the barbarians far across the world.

.

## Weaving a Web

A spider is working diligently before me
this Sunday morning. Long silken threads stretch
out, waving in each gust of air.
Only a burst of unexpected light reveals the intricate,
ever- changing pattern. Its skill lies in
its invisibility so that we can walk
through our morning without seeing
its creation as we turn our attention
to the World Cup soccer match. Meanwhile
Imam Abu Omar is snatched from the sidewalk
as he walks home from his mosque in Milan,
vanished in the web that stretches
from Cairo to Amman, to Timisoara, Kabul,
Islamabad and Guantanamo. No one ever
sees this network of secret *renditions*
and detentions, an underworld
that pulses beneath our *secured* houses:
thousands hurled outside of time.

# We Are Making Progress

Suddenly the power goes out
in the very last art gallery in Iraq.
The temperature rises
to 100 degrees Fahrenheit.

There will be no exhibit
today. Just a few artists
have gathered, those
who have not fled.

Noori al-Rawi* cries out
*I haven't picked up*
*a paintbrush in two years.*
*I want to burn my art history archives,*

*rip my heart out.*
Hasan, the self-proclaimed
curator of what remains,
is one of the last to believe

in tomorrow.  There are no more

hallowed spaces; golden domes

where hearts once soared

are shattered, neighborhoods


and villages are shuffled

like cards, a whole country in exile

within its own borders.

Here even the clouds bleed.

*

Mr. Rawi, one of the pioneers of Iraqi
modern art, is also a curator and art scholar
who founded 4 art museums in Baghdad.

## My Country

At the palace a heightened alert.
It seems the enemy is everywhere.
If we are afraid,
We will stop trusting our eyes,
our steps that carry us through the day's
rough terrain. Our hands will forget
the kingdom of touch, we'll rein in
our voices, stop sending thoughts
that would bind us together across oceans,
beyond mountains.

But a moment can redeem us:
a dove piercing the morning air
with its *hoo hoo*, a pair of monarch butterflies
swooping and weaving in tremulous
foreplay, then soaring above the trees,
reminding us that we too are citizens
of the sky, the wind, the light.

# What Words Can Do

*for James Wright*

As he scans the list
of battle-frayed soldiers,
the officer shrugs.
Their night sweats,
their inner numbness
are a foreign language to him.
*No longer of use*
is what he doesn't say.
But in a small town up North
a college president walks out
of his kingdom of books
and humming classes,
across neatly mowed lawns
and into hospital wards
where days keep collapsing
in the corridors. A former marine,
he comes with his own
memories, speaking the language

of tremors, nightmares

and invisible wounds.

He moves from one

bed to another,

holding each patient

with his words. He turns these

words into ladders

the maimed can climb up

and out into the world again.

## One Body

From the horses in the meadow shuddering off flies

to the insects nesting beneath tree bark

to the bracero and his children

in the harsh forests of corn

to the man wielding his scythe in the tall grass

and the small children at play,

their loose hair indistinguishable

from the field flowers,

the whole world is one body.

Dawn embraces even those

who claim to stand apart:

commandos ramming their bulldozers

into olive groves and peaceful houses

because they were near the border,

and the ones who hide among us

dragging naked prisoners

along the dank corridors of their laughter.

# Brazzaville

Her fathomless eyes hold me —
the Congolese woman in her hospital bed,
stump of a leg swathed
in white, stump of one arm
swathed in white so we cannot see
the wounds, the bullets gone wild,
or hear the thunk of ax
against bone. So we cannot see the forest
bruised by marauding soldiers,
or the wisp of smoke
that was once a village —
what she will always see.

# Sudan

*for Diagne Chanel*

The ones who survived cannot speak
of their anguish. It would be like touching
live coals. Those who walk on firm ground
would not understand what it is
to cross raging waters without a bridge.
Those scenes remain locked in their throats
forever scalding their dreams. And what of the thousands
slaughtered like prey, their throats slit,
a wilderness of young and old
tangled in mounds. They have not disappeared.
Their gaze follows us everywhere
asking, why did you turn away?

## In Praise of Flowers

While the world thunders around me,
the vision of my granddaughter's face,
wearing a sadness beyond her years —

I gather hibiscus, grateful for the bright
galaxies of pollen on their pistils,
for their delicate sexual tongues igniting the air.

While children are gently stirring from sleep
in Basra only to be torn from
their houses by flying mortar,

and while rich nations turn away
from the children withering
in their mother's arms in Niger,

I arrange pale pinks, deep mauves,
yellows and burnt orange in shallow bowls,
honoring the blossoms' brief passage.

To awaken to the mysteries of the flowers

each day is a way of remembering

how the world devours its children

from New Orleans to Kashmir.

The yellow silky petals seem like the only

angel wings among us.

# Equipoise

In the basement of the museum
glass cases throb with porcelains
from the Ming Dynasty. A Taoist priest stares
gravely at his text, a barbarian
tears at his ragged hair.

I pause before a woman
with an almost liquid veil
falling behind her shoulders, balancing a child
on her hip, her forehead an oasis
of serenity. Meanwhile

bombs explode in London,
leaving holes larger than canyons
in families who kissed their loved ones goodbye
only an hour before.

I think of the woman holding her child,

the Goddess of Compassion.

*Is anything unrelated in this world?*

# Step by Step

*for Preah Maha Ghosananda*

Hands folded, head bowed,
he would walk the narrow paths
through jungles, the ground
still sown with landmines
at the edges of trails.
Step by step he journeyed,
his glasses fogged, his hitched-up monk's robes
tangled in bushes. Behind him
trudged rows and rows of chanting
monks and nuns. Sometimes
shells screamed above
and firefights exploded on either side.
Sometimes they joined streams of refugees
alongside ox-carts piled high with mattresses
and caged chickens.
*We must find the courage*
*to leave our temples*

*and enter the suffering-filled temples*

*of human experience.* How else to reach

a man digging his fields,

the woman bent over the river washing,

a lone soldier hoisting his rifle?

Step by step, to spread the Metta Sutta,

the words of love, healing

the martyred decades of Cambodia.

# The Hymn Beginning and Ending with Our Naked Flesh

# Faith

When I was young, I pummeled doors
until cracks appeared just wide
enough to slip through only to discover
more fortified gates. Now, in the tight
confines of illness, when the lockup
stretches into years, the air beyond the bars
is thick with learned discourse, there are preachers
who confound their images
with God's, bureaucracies that douse
themselves with incense.

I unroll my prayer rug
and face East. I take out my loom
and doves flutter among
blossoming trees. I call out
and sometimes distant bells
resonate below sound, I see a holy man
on the sidewalk below.

With time, the doors keep
opening within me. Here I plant
fields of wheat, walk through
my yesterdays, hold eternity
in a newborn's curled hands.

## March Rain

No sleep last night and a bone chilling rain
this morning. Instead of the sun's
reassuring arms, only bare trees
weeping. But maybe this gray sky
that is so blank, so toneless
is waiting for someone
to really gaze at it, to startle
the silent birds. It is raining this morning
but how can we possibly predict
when and where true happiness
comes. It hides among the books
on my desk, in the tear stained
branches at my window.
It hides in the memory
of my husband's words when I cried out
I could go no farther. "You must try,"
he murmured, "You must try
because you are precious."
In this bone chilling rain

of my illness, in the numbing

gray skies, a single word

opened a horizon, a road

where I could walk.

## Always

I want to keep you with me
always, you say, more and more often


now when days blur past like the mountain stream
where we lingered one afternoon


as it hurtled over rocks,
now when summer's green slopes


are awakening and the air
braided by swallows. The silence cradling


us with its fullness seems to cancel
the discarded armaments


of ski-lifts, the commerce of electric wires,
the wars boiling through our windows,

the sappers and bombers. Oh, now when
we are surrounded by the eternity of drenched

fields, we can hear woodpeckers
drilling the seconds on iron tree trunks.

# Maui

In late afternoon teenage boys with surf- boards hurl
themselves
in the waves, couples stroll along the shore
as if they were skirting the edge of the world
where the sky's drunken beauty trails
sun-shot clouds. The beach is alive with the smell
of wood fire and grilled fish, with children
thwacking a ball back and forth across a net.
But a man with tangled hair walks though this scene
like a shadow, shreds of tattered shorts
clinging to his thighs. I have seen him before,
a bush of black hair through the crowds
as he walks doggedly back and forth
without a destination, the pages of his life
written in a language only he can read. His loneliness
swallows me and I think how our walls
are never high enough to keep out the stench
of misery, how the world lays its palm,
on my heart like a burning coal.

# Reprieve

As we walked by the ocean at dusk,
the waves slipped in with the shush
of rustling silk. There was no thunder
of breakers against the rocks,
no trucks rumbled by with music
thudding from open windows.
There were only a few fishermen
quietly lowering their nets,
tending their lines.

The wind, had gone
elsewhere. For a moment
the headlines retreated: the killings
in the Sudan, the car bombs
in Basra and that other war
where children are sold into slavery
because of hunger.

For a moment
the world held its breath.

# Where They Put You

*for Blanche Boulanger*

People are coming in and out of focus,
through the lens you can't adjust
when we walk through the door
of Aldridge House. The light swims
in your eyes, you are glad we are here.
*How nice to be with you again,*
you smile as if we had stepped
out of years, although
it has only been days.

\* \* \*

*Do I have a home?* you ask,
knowing somehow that this featureless
room is not a room
to live in but someplace
temporary like a train
only a train stuck
in its tracks, the seats

all the same, the aisles busy
with strangers. *Who put me here?*
you insist. I try to tell you
how, when, why
but all you want
is yes or no
all you want is the truth.

\* \* \*

I call you Blanchette
as your mother once did
in Grenoble, hoping to bring
you back to yourself.
You are not here
at this anonymous table
you never set, before plates
that appear and disappear.
You are not here,
but suddenly you tell me,
*My parents had a restaurant*
*in Grenoble you know, that's why*
*I was never interested in food.*

\* \* \*

I cannot bring you
back to where you do not
wish to go; to remember
that once you had a husband,
once it was you who arranged the flowers
on the altar for Easter,
you who took care of all the accounts.
I clasp you in my arms
as if I were leaving
you at the terminal
and there was only one minute left.

# Maud

As if you knew it would be the last

time, the stories of your early childhood poured out:

how 3 brothers and 3 sisters shared

one bed by sleeping in different directions,

the small pleasures of a rare meat stew,

a day without chores, a ramble along

the Northern coast. You had just turned

90, presiding over the tidy kingdom

of your council flat, the curtains

you sewed despite your fading

eyesight, photos of your great-grandchildren

illuminating the mantel, your garden

of plants on the miniature terrace

and that note you taped on the fridge,

"Just do it!" before that slogan

became popular. My buoyant 6- year- old

granddaughter, your great-granddaughter,

sat close beside you as she listened

while you recounted your world

in the high pitched tone of the deaf.

Later we took photos of the two of you,

your arm encircling her. Months after you died,

my granddaughter announced,

"great-gran can see and hear now,"

with that deeper knowing you passed down.

# What Remains

*for Lucie Bouvard*

Time has swallowed your house at Fontenay-sous-Bois
with its rich furniture: the silver cups for cherry brandy
handed round after dinner, the long white curtains
billowing in the dining-room where you sat
at the head of the table, the kitchen
with its gleaming appliances where you spun potatoes
into mounds of gold, and the drawers
with silk scarves and necklaces
you wore with such pride. You reigned in that space,
your family swaying like willows
beneath your tempests or your smiles.
That house is empty now,
the rugs rolled up and shipped
to the four corners of the world by the army
of the living. Not even an echo remains.
But in the handkerchief I carry in my purse,
the one embroidered with delicate blue flowers
you brought back from Switzerland,

your heart still flutters, released now

from the tyranny of the scepter.

# After Maillol

## Night

Night strides across borders.
Hush, she commands the barking dogs,
the searchlights, the buckling barbed
wire fences. She cradles
the earth in her gleaming limbs
until the only sounds are those of mingled
breaths, the quick intake of the child's,
the drawn out sobs of the aged
and the ill. Beneath her steady wings
soldiers dream of tilling fields,
prison doors slide open.

## Spring

Spring is slender-limbed,
offering her nakedness, the music
of frail petals opening. She calls to us
among our books and papers,
a sudden wash of light spilling

into our day. We pause,

remembering how the screen door

clanged as we sailed

into morning, the scent

of our first lover's skin.


Grief

The sea ebbs and flows through

Grief's body, its cargo jerking beyond

her hands. She is always the first

and the last: the battlefield opens

on her doorstep, hunger knocks

at her window. She knows there are no differences

between the children of this world,

the new ones and the fully grown, that the sorrow

she carries in her massive arms

is our common language.

# The Second Tide

Her parents and grandparents vanished into the giant maw.
Now she wanders with nothing between her

and the sky, no roof, no arms to enfold her,
 no clatter of pots as her mother once bent

over the cooking fire, and chickens fluttered
in the doorway, no village paths

to follow. Now is the time of vultures circling
with promises who will take her to foreign cities

where she will lose her name, where she will be locked away,
to be ravaged by blank-faced men, swallowed

in the second tide of those who disappeared,
leaving us with songs of grief, the only possible music.

# The Door Across the Street

During the last months, he wandered
through the house, ashen-faced,
dozing in front of the television
or calling out to his wife.
She thought she could hold him
with chicken soup and protein shakes,
tempt him with car rides.
She thought she could keep him
coiled in the tense thread
of her love. She knew and didn't
know how the last door
would swing open as the men
arrived with a stretcher
strapping him in until only
his bare feet and his mouth
were open to the night sky
while she kept screaming
as if she were falling

and there was nothing
to hold her up.

## Coming Home

Under the spring rain, everything
is liquid: the bird calls, the branches'
languid sweep. Under this sky
with its conjugating grays, the greens

are more intense, the larks
are jubilant. The earth inhales me,
the earth that will finally embrace me.
When I unbuckle my skin,

I want to be by the lake
where I walked with my love
year after year as we wrote
our own story. I want the blessing

of *earth to earth*, not the baleful
intoning of *dust to dust*.
We were so much more than that.
We shone like the orange lichen

starring the woods. My children

and my grandchildren do not need to wander

among stones. I will be there waiting

for them when they come home.

# Praise

I love the dusk inside churches,
the soft glow seeping
through windows, most of all
when the pulpit is silent and my thoughts
not drowned out.

My reverence is for the perfect
body of a newborn, all the wayward tendrils
of growth, the butterflies' drunken wing beats
in a lavender field, leaves gathering
moisture above arid fields.

An olive tree flames in my breast,
its aged trunk scarred by wind,
leaves rushing upward.
Its songs are the cicadas'
fugues, the joyous shrieks
of children playing in its shade.

I want to overthrow the papacy,

bulldoze rectories where penitents

cherish hair shirts, edifices where the powerful

listen to themselves in airless rooms.

I want to praise speaking

out of turn, fling open the doors

to outcasts, honor the fragile body's

wisdom, the unpredictability of light.

## Sister Water

Mountain streams thunder into lakes
and reservoirs; melts hurtle
down the slopes in silver veins,
spangling pastures with gentians
and alpenrose. This is the longed for
season when driving up into the green
spaciousness and glistening rocks
is also a tumbling down, when stones
are thatched with miniature blooms.
Water regenerates the earth
of ourselves— *sister water*, St. Francis
called it— a roaring in the ears,
the snow banks giving way, carved
from within, body against body
rinsed in their own light.

# Our Lady of Guadelupe

*Sin*, the padre intones. *Christ loved us*
*more than his own body, and yet*
*we are sinners, we forget how he died.*
The padre points to the blood-stained
torso on the altar. But on the wall
La Guadelupina glows. She is in a field
with the dust swirling, the air
both cool and burning. She is the Mother
who wears our face, whose words
are the smoothest sun-warmed stones.
She alights, almost touching
the ground and we rise a little
with our supplicant hands.
She is wrapped in the blueness
of sky, telling us that she loves
the multi-colored earth of ourselves.

## Isabella

My granddaughter has the black
diamond shaped eyes of a Cherokee.
When she smiles they blaze

in the white and pink
rose of her face. Isabella who carries
so many countries in her veins

also bears unclaimed geographies.
One afternoon when she was barely two years old
and the adults were wrapped in conversation,

Isabella danced the way light vibrates
on water, her red dress blurring.
She whirled on the electric currents

of her great-great-grandmothers who knew
that every moment on this earth
is sacred and must be praised, who surround

her with their chants as she carries

them in her knowing eyes,

the forest of her black hair.

# After

*for Jean B.*

It's like this: when we slip out of bone
and flesh, we also shed the anger,
the strife, the times we failed to speak
with grace and times we failed to listen
to each other. We take off
the blindness that wants us to be
always the center.


I saw it in a dream even before
the cancer finally took him —
he whom we knew as harsh
and unfeeling. –– his face
suffused with light, his once sullen mouth
rinsed with joy.

# What Time Can Do

Suddenly you are in a forest
of skin-scent, tongue, lightening
eyes, the way she spoke
with her hands, guided needles
through quilts, scribbled notes
on odd bits of paper at all hours
yet raged at computers,
machines in general,
how she threaded the day
ushering in evening
with a canticle of plates
and glasses, the latest news
unfurling above a tureen.
And then a sheaf of dark hair
splayed on the pillow beside you.
She wanted to recount the day
from the beginning, to walk
in suppositions while you drifted
in and out of sleep the way we do

in this life with moments

of awakening when we stumble

headlong into the landscape of memory.

# The Years

You walk with one foot in winter's black ice, the other

in a burgeoning meadow. Can joy

and sadness co-exist? You've traveled

through years; the precincts of rebellion,

despair and fulfillment but you can still be moved

by a few violets shyly spreading

their colors, a caterpillar turning the earth.

Age has honed you down

to opposite poles: the narrowing

of your perimeters and the mysterious cosmos

of the heart. Soon your voice will be

only a dim echo. But the world will go on

with its noise. Chieftains will try

to herd us in small spaces, new voices

stake out their refusal, and passion

flare in quiet alleys. There will always be

unexpected moments of astonishment.

# Only on this Earth

Only on this earth, our naked bodies
entwined in a silence suffused with years
of tenderness and knowing
as if we were the holy dusk
of a cathedral, the one we visited
in Venasque last summer:

Outside the white- hot fields were drenched
with lavender and cicadas, inside
I heard the echoes of so many lives
that passed through these walls: Longobards
and Celts, Goths and Franks.

Only on this earth, the endless migration
of peoples, the mingling of blood,
your language and mine
transmuted. Only on this harrowed earth,
our bodies the illuminated book
of hours with harvests and droughts, hands

filled and emptied — our mingled breath

so alive, yet holding

our vanishing, the way cathedrals

enfold their empty spaces,

the hymn beginning and ending

with our naked flesh.

# View from the Future

# Ariel

Granddaughter, I am dreaming you
into this world. You are wearing
my singlet of eggs, my banners
of prayer. I am dreaming my grandmother
walking beside you as she adjusts
her lorgnettes. My great-grandmother
rustles in wafting the scent
of lindens from Senoseccia.
All the grandmothers are keeping watch,
their words hovering like wings,
so you will draw the wisdom
of different continents, the consonance
of many languages, so you will remember
stars, galaxies and solar winds
when you enter the blue dome of breath.

# In Transit

## 1

I arrived here on a river
of thorns, harsh mother
who taught me
how to invent mornings, how to
clear paths in the thickets
of my head.

## 2

I threaded my way among
travelers pulling their carry-ons
and speaking on cell phones, their faces
shuttered, their steps erased
by the crush of other steps.
I skirted a woman struggling
with her cane. Mine
was invisible.

3

Now in this green kingdom
I listen to the grass telling
its stories to the rain as if it too
had just arrived and was busy
unrolling its parchment
of roots and wings.

# River in Spring

*After a painting by Francis Brooks Chadwick*

This is what life is meant to be, pulling us
beyond the countertop littered
with dishes, the desk that awaits us
each morning with a certainty we both
long for and dread, beyond the medicine bottles
lined up by the sickbed – this turquoise river
shimmering before us, the trees along
its banks, not green but a deep ochre,
each quivering with its own intensity, flinging
bronze shadows on the water, the clumps
of purple tipped reeds erupting
like brushfires — this is what draws us
beyond ourselves, the strong gestures,
the refusal to be defined, the longing to always push
at the limits in search of the awakening
the return to miracle.

# St. John in the Desert

When he went into the desert
Saint John brought only his staff
and his hunger to its hallucination
of plains and valleys. As the days lost
their markings, the air
quivered with his thoughts,
the world opened
its scars, voices pierced
his dreams. Yet he stayed
where there was no path,
no green leaf, only the wind
of his torment, only his staff.

## Learning to Read

The lake is steeped
in meditation, gray silk

furrowed by sun-shot
clouds, the drowned

firs holding their breath.
We walk over pine needles

and dried leaves as we have
always walked

but never so drawn
into the somber glory

of these woods, oaks lifting
their naked arms, lichen

starring the gnawed off

stumps—as if we were


reading breviaries

of yielding, of becoming.

## Easter Sunday

A small fire sputtered in the wind
as the priest raised his arm  in benediction
chanting "Holy Fire," then bent down
 to light the Easter candle,
his billowing robes just missing the flames.
We filed inside the church
lighting each other's candles,
my breast thrumming
with expectation.


But then a loud-voiced woman
opened the book of Genesis
The world was created
*in seven days*, she began.
I wanted to stand
and shout at her that outside
the stained glass windows
the Blue-Ridge mountains
were moving downwards through eons

while the Rockies were still
thrusting skywards.

But for God there was no time,
there was no inside
or outside. God was in forgiveness
and in the child wailing
in his mother's arms as if she knew
what life would bring. God was in the flapping
wings of our off-key voices,
and while we bowed
our heads, He stoked
the great roaring fire
of all that is silent and unseen.

## Vivaldi's L'Estro Harmonico

You named it *l'estro*, meaning fertile, say egg
from which the earth opens
and your strings pour forth a dazzle
of rushing wings, balance stars
on bows. You, asthmatic

who gasped for breath,
turned illness into a bird poised on a cross wind,
trilling its colors
for the sheer joy of it.

Red headed priest, your bones lie
in a pauper's grave,
but your violin still soars
beyond the flash floods of Venetian disdain
and the sudden death of your patron,

still utters its harmonies above the turbulence
of fortune and misfortune

as it opens its lips,

its burnished throat, its lavish tongue.

# Under the Rain

*for Brad*

The lilacs, the fields are dripping
like fresh canvases. Under the close
gray sky, the grass takes on
its deeper hues revealing yellows,
and cobalt blues, the earth turns ochre.
Under the rain

     our silences assume
their own colors: my friend disabled
steers his electric scooter
through city streets surrounded
by green. His hands
grasping the bars, spill
flowers. Rain
washes over the roads

     and we are visible
again. The selves we pronounce

in crowded rooms are hushed

as the heart strides out

proclaiming its greens

and ochres, its burnt orange.

# Cluses

is a small mountain town with lyric fountains
and green squares, a main street
spangled with *parfumeries, patisseries artisanales*,
shop windows blooming with low cut dresses
where elegant young blondes stroll with their children
in tow. But everything is changing. On the back streets
*Kabobs* is splayed on the windows of the cafés,
and women in chadors hang out their laundry
on cluttered terraces. There's a Carrefour,
the French Wal-Mart, a city in itself
where the aisles seem to stretch towards
infinity, and boredom and detachment
are written on the cashiers' faces.
You drive there past Place Charles de Gaulle
and the Avenue de la Libération. But there's only one
history although everything is changing.
And although the mountains spread their wings,
there's no room for Orhan, Fazil, Nazim or Saleh
who hang out in the street behind the store

in their black tee shirts and shaved heads,

teenagers caught between two worlds,

wanting to be visible, wanting to have their say.

# Names

Zoe Mogilnitsky sits next to me in Latin Class,
a tangled cloud of pale hair, profile cut from
the magical stone of a far off country. I remember
how she smiled with delight as if the world were all
windows and doors, even when I received the prize
for Latin. I didn't understand why our teacher
scowled at Zoe until her face seemed to crumble.
Later I met her in college. "I'm Zoe Mogil
now," she said smiling, but quieter.

*

"Margarita Anna Earnesta Frederika Cornelia,
Maria, that's my whole name," I announce with pride.
My classmates stare at me, then laugh, "that's too
many, they can't all be yours." My grandmother could
explain, but she's at home, waiting for me with her
stories of wars and empires and I'm in the country of
people with no yesterdays, where nobody want to know.

*

Krishna, Yaweh, Buddha, Allah, stupas, temples,
cathedrals, ashrams, but when I'm in the museum caught
in the light of Turkish miniatures, my heart turns over
before a panel of vibrant black characters, "God," they
flash even before I read the translation. And when
the morning dove's whoo whoo sounds its tocsin beneath
my breastbone, it's God's voice in the body's nave, his
wings stirring the breath that speaks all languages.

# Jae

*Petite goutte d'eau* your great uncle calls you
because you are a drop in the middle
of the vast field of your parents' bed,

drop of water that harbors all colors,
where light quivers and expands.
When your black eyes crinkle at the edges

you are an emperor decreeing laughter.
With tiny fingers you topple the bright
nesting cups: the grandmother

who disappeared one night, slipping away
through a back alley in Soeul,
the grandfather who thought he lost

only a war and his years,
and your mother who was abandoned,
who wept because she was like no one

in this world. Carefully you fit them

back together, you wave your hands

with glee. Little acorn


who carries the long shadows of trees,

*petite goutte d'eau,* mirror

in which your mother comes home.

# View from the Future

Everything is out of sequence:
We wake from a dream of snow banks,
when suddenly the weeping cherry
bursts into flame, the fields
are blanketed

      in fierce light. Summer
erupts before spring, children
shoot their classmates in a schoolyard,
children kill each other in streets.
What begins as a slight explodes
like a mine in an abandoned field.
The word abandonment

      is what I mean. The politicians
loom on television and then return
to airless rooms. Nothing
has changed and everything; the slow
progression of seasons, the children,

aimless and invisible.
We want to stop

      this burning down
but our leaders announce the earth
is still on course.

# Invading the Mountain in Combloux

They felt nothing as they
gouged into the pasture's soft
body, tearing away layer
after layer, dismantling
the stillness. When they were finished
they lit up their cigarettes
and roared off in their trucks.
Now, there will be no mornings,
just the sharp glare of light
against asphalt. There will be
no hushed twittering of birds,
 no stamping of hooves
or distant jangle of cow bells.
 They have assassinated the breath
of freshness, the green flames washing the air,
the odors of dung and flowers.
There will be no slow awakening,
drifting into consciousness
with a pulsing chorus of secret voices,

a tender vibrato of leaves

and crickets. There will be no changing

colors. One day will become

just like another. We will move

more quickly, exiled

to a country where there will be

no refuge from ourselves.

# Elegy for a Mustard Field

On Old Stage Coach road, markers wave
their blue and orange flags
and a house is emptied, stripped
of its clapboard.

Now, the woman won't take her apron
from its hook to usher in the day,
and the dog will no longer
worry the chickens.

The hawks won't keep watch
on their corridors of air
or the bees stake out their
kingdoms on the locust tree.

Now the hollow behind the house
is swamped by silence, pocked
with tree stumps where weeping cherries
once spread their incandescence.

A bypass cancelled the simple acts

of mowing, of caulking fissures

above the doorway

and sweeping the porch —


extinguishing the lives inside,

that were so singular

yet unremarked.

# Chloe

I passed a young girl in the street
yesterday. Her black hair brushed her face
like wings. Her jeans sat low
on her hips as she walked with her friends.

> Is that what tore you away from us,
> the empty space where there should have been
> friends?

I passed a young boy and his father on the street
yesterday. The father was white.
The boy had café-au-lait skin
and unsure eyes.

.

> Is that what tore you away from us, the mirror
> that didn't show your face?

Did the streets diminish you, streets without
women in rebozos or stalls of fresh fruit?

Is that what tore you away from us?

Everyone so sure of themselves, the corridors
at school, the neat houses and lawns, the everydayness
of chatter swirling around you.

Did it silence the tremulous whispering
inside your heart?

You who already considered the plain facts
of absence fell headlong into its gorge
too soon

      not knowing that we too would drown
      in our own eyes night after night.

# My Town

Summers it is the kingdom of trees,
pin oak, sugar maple, linden,
and copper beech spread their shining
umbrellas over the streets. Islands
of flowerbeds wave us to the center of town
and its proud library,

      But few read the phosphorescent
blue-green around the pine studded lake,
or remember Lizzie with her long blond hair,
her face puckered by prednisone, or Jim
who used to pass the collection plate at church,
or Annie who at seventeen, lost her womb
and so many futures. They left in a hush, their names
carted away with the leaves.

      Open our newspaper and you will see
the litany of houses for sale; perfect
for "sophisticated living." The subtext

is hidden; the phosphorescent blue-green,

the plumes traveling underground

near the wells like unexploded bombs.

# Redbud

On this wheel the soldier who defected

during the Civil War and who died of hunger

in the brush is now inscribed near

the general who carried the banner

to victory. The man sitting in his rocking

chair on the observatory of his porch

while warriors invaded

far off countries to the boom of cannons –

appears in the same whorl. Where conquerors strode

and cities rose and crumbled,

all gather now in chapters of silence.

# Le Mistral

*The Mistral is a marauding wind that periodically*
*sweeps down on Provence in gusts without warning.*

For nine days olive trees shimmered
and writhed, stately blue pines
dipped and swayed, strands of oaks
galloped in place and the grasses flew by
like a streak of tigers. Everywhere
clumps of genet rose in fiery tongues
scattering their blossoms' wild perfume.
Earth was on the move again, the wind
spiraling from the Alps through
the Rhone Valley, reclaiming
Provence with its lavender fields,
its hilltop villages and limestone houses.
The Mistral uttered its prophetic chants
as the plane trees with their time- scarred
trunks commenced their ritual dance, wearing
evening's gilded robes, rattling their gourds,
their voices stilling ours.

## Antonio Gaudi's Cathedral

He want us to see so much, to love
so intensely, let our eccentricities bloom.
Like a grandfather coaxing his young ones
towards the future, he tells us
not to be timid of cowed, not to sit

on the sidelines of the feast, to to exult
with the stone, the hosannahs of leaves
and towers. He wants us to multiply
our hands like the coral, let the sky nest
on our balconies, welcome the fishes of light

among the wrought iron kelp.
He wants us to open with windows
like the yawn of some fantastic dolphin.
If only we would read the book
of nature, we would see that no wind blusters

between East and West, no fence rises

between one nature and another, between animal,

mineral or plant. We would see

that like his spires, the mountains

really tilt. We would walk under the slanted palms

of his arches, plunge through corridors

as if we were swimming underwater

or through the heart of the earth, as it is –

as we could be —- not tamed or bent by the world,

but passionate as molten rock.

## As Dusk Fell

She was turning the pages of a book.
Outside her window the trees
were weaving a sky of trembling
purples and reds. Voices rose from the pages
like cicadas charting the direction
of wind and the dimension of fields.
outside her window the leaves
were singing as if they were birds
signaling departure. The pages of her book
burned with all she held
within her heart, children sweeping
through the chapters like comets,
the faces of her forbears surfacing like
coins in newly plowed furrows
in Acquilea. Turning the pages she saw
corridors of rain, how even though
her book was slender it held such mysteries.
She was turning its pages
as dusk fell and larks twittered

sleepily, turning, as the stars
flung out their crystal banners.
She dreamed she was walking
behind her mother in a space so vast,
a mountain so steep, she was afraid,
remembering all that would be erased.

# The Important Thing

is to give with abandon
and when you are the most naked, so that your hunger
turns into fields of gleaming fruit trees
and your frail and aging body
harbors a spirit that dwarfs mountains,
so that your giving is a path
towards endless vistas like the dying man
telling his art student
during her very last visit, "If only
I had a few pears I could paint."
She thought it was to assuage
her grief, yet when he died, the pears
began to bloom on her canvases
with the quivering of new flesh, the sad
flames of sunset, the translucence
of tears. Like the woman in a Hungarian
prison whose birthday gift
to her cell mate was a rose made
out of toilet paper, a flower that survived

her execution. The important thing
is to give, randomly
and out of poverty, not knowing
whether the heart's pale shoots
will create leaves or perish.

Marguerite Guzmán Bouvard was for many years a professor of Political Science and director of poetry workshops at Regis College, and has been a writer in residence at the University of Maryland. She is multidisciplinary and has published 16 books, including 6 books of poetry, and numerous articles in the fields of Political Science, Psychology, Spirituality, Literature and Poetry. Both her poetry and essays have been widely anthologized. She has received fellowships at the Radcliffe Institute and the Wellesley College Center for Research on Women and grants for her poetry from the Puffin and the Danforth foundations. She is a Resident Scholar at the Women Studies Research Center, Brandeis University.

Printed in the United States
210017BV00001B/100/P